PROUD TO BE

A PRIDE POETRY COLLECTION

EDITED BY JK LARKIN

Copyright © 2023

All rights reserved.

Published by Red Penguin Books

Bellerose Village, New York

No part of this book may be reproduced in any form or by any electronic or mechanical means, including information storage and retrieval systems, without written permission from the author, except for the use of brief quotations in a book review.

CONTENTS

PRIDE March Penn	1
CHALLAH IF YOU QUEER ME Allison Fradkin	3
I LOVE LEZZIE Allison Fradkin	5
SALSA JAR TRIOLET Mariel Cariker	7
THE DAY WE FIRST MET Linda M. Crate	9
HOW TO FLIRT Gregg Shapiro	11
MISS CUED Allison Fradkin	13
BECAUSE OF FACEBOOK Gregg Shapiro	17
THE BOY Mykyta Ryzhykh	19
THE NEW STANDARD Scott Wiggerman	21
ACHING Benny Varotta	23
A LITTLE QUEER, TOO Linda M. Crate	25
REALITY Abdulrazaq Salihu	27
BLEEDING HEARTS Chris Biles	29
ASYLUM SEEKER Scott Wiggerman	31
NO SAY Chris Biles	33
CHAOS IN THE COSMOS Chris Biles	35
RESURRECTION Scott Wiggerman	37

PERMA-VALENTINE Celia McClure	39
EVEN IF NO APOLOGY WILL EVER BE ENOUGH Linda M. Crate	41
LONG KISS Scott Wiggerman	43
GROWTH//DECAY Celia McClure	45
SEPARATION Alice Rose	47
WE WAKE UP IN THE SUMMER Celia McClure	49
MY TRUE IDENTITY Linda M. Crate	51
GAY PRIDE Scott Wiggerman	53
THE DYKE-CLARATION OF LESBI-INDEPENDENCE Allison Fradkin	55
MY QUEER GENERATION Maid Čorbić	57
HEAR ME OUT Allison Fradkin	59
SCARLET Benny Varotta	61
REVERENCE FOR THEIR LAVENDER VALIANCE Bob McNeil	63
WHAT RETURNS? Mariel Cariker	65
About the Authors	67
Also from The Red Penguin Collection	71

"If you are not personally free to be yourself in that most important of all human activities – the expression of love – then life loses its meaning."

– Harvey Milk

PRIDE

- March Penn

I asked the man at the *Gertrude Stein Democratic Club*
if he liked Gertrude Stein, and he said,
Oh Honey, This club is for gay democrats. How are you?

All belly belly well. Not exactly.
Yes, exactly presently as exactly...
I wondered whether that's true

or, if inside, I kept splitting into different presences,
the desire to write a queer poem
becoming a poem about wanting connection

and about the family members who have given up on connection.
I feel more strange to still believe in romance than to be queer.

Hey, look at that girl, a passing driver says,
She's talking to herself. See how she's gesturing with her hands.

CHALLAH IF YOU QUEER ME

- *Allison Fradkin*

    Everything I need to know about being Jewish I learned from *The Nanny*:
                  Every meshugeneh needs a mensch
                Don't schlep—get married already!
                 If you're over thirty and single
                      you might be—
                      —it's likely—
                        you're gay
                        (Oy vey!)
            There'll be kvetching and kibitzing
            You'll become a Jewcy bit of gossip
          People will say pish, you're just *farmisht*
                Your mishpochah will plotz
             Start packing for your guilt trip
                  (Guilt: Just Jew it)

                But what if you can't forget
           about that little matzo ball of fire
               you met at the synagogue
             The one with charm and chutzpah
     who makes your eyes light up like a menorah
             your head spin like a dreidel
          and your heart chant *Hava Nagila*
              every time you look at her

                  For Hashem's sake
                  —and your own—
            don't let some schmendricks
              rain on your pride parade
      or make you feel like schmutz on a schmatte
  or pressure you to take their verkakte-mamie advice:
     At least date a non-goy boy before you make it official!

Instead, get them to kiss your keppie like everything's kosher,

because wonder of wonder,
queer-acle of queer-acles,
it is

So trade that guilt for (chocolate) gelt
break out the bubbly grape juice
and propose a toast:
to life
to love
to loving your life
and the *meydl* with the *sheyn ponem* in it
Your chosen person
Your finest Frantasy

Just do it with justifiable Jewbilance

I LOVE LEZZIE

- Allison Fradkin

It all started during a vacation from marriage.
Not mine—Lucy Ricardo's.
Naturally, Ethel takes a hiatus
from her husband too,
and Lucy moves in with
—though not in on—
her gal pal.
But all hope is not lost,
least of all when Lucy lets loose
with this loaded remark: *I hope you boys
are going to have as gay an evening
as we are.*
(You know, they really were pioneer women, those two,
what with all the accidental advocating they did
for marriage equality.)

Okay, so maybe that remark really wasn't so gay,
given the time period in which it was uttered,
but I chose to take it the right way:
as permission to
define,
refine,
and redefine
my sexuality.
I could do more than identify
as a member
of the LGBT community.
I could ident-defy:
as
Liberated,
Grateful,
Bodacious,
and Tenacious.

Seeing this revelation
as cause for celebration,
I went singin' in the rainbow
that I prefer dolls to guys.
Mama said there'll be gays like this:
those who embrace their sexuality straight away,
not only because they've figured out
that the bloom is off the heteros;
but also because,
in the words of midcentury chanteuse Dinah Washington,
What a diff'rence a gay makes
or, you know, something a little more fifties-friendly
like:
I love lezzie and she loves me
Queer as happy as two can be…

SALSA JAR TRIOLET

- Mariel Cariker

"You know I am crazy about you."
and your eyes go soft.
You look at me like I'm new.
"You know I am crazy about you."
Calloused my hands like
a cap I've tried my hardest to unscrew
and I reach for you
looking for warm water
for help.
"You know I am totally crazy about you."
and your eyes go soft.

THE DAY WE FIRST MET

i remember her softness,
the curve of her curls;
kind and trembling voice—

was a bit disappointed
that her pictures weren't turning
out quite right,
said she felt cute but the
camera didn't agree;
i whispered: "but you are cute"—

don't think she heard me,
though,
she gave me a soft sad smile

before she ordered her food;

had myself a crush and was a bit
tongue tied,
but i never saw her again—

sometimes i still wonder about that
girl with her yellow rain jacket,
and i hope she is happier
than the day we first met.

- *linda m. crate*

HOW TO FLIRT

- *Gregg Shapiro*

Listen to Doris Day singing, "Once I had a secret
love," no more than 214 times a day or an amount
equal to your heartbeat on an especially loathsome
or love-soaked Valentine's Day when you were nine
or nineteen years old. Avoid singing or humming

"Que Sera Sera" like a cheating ex. Otherwise
"whatever will be" won't be. Bat your eyes but try
not to think about baseball bats, Christian Bale

as Batman, vampire bats or batty old ladies like
Aunt Clara on "Bewitched." Be bewitching without
twitching or casting an irreversible spell. Spell it out
in letters big enough to read from a great distance.
Keep your distance from boxes of chocolates, bouquets

of flowers, anything associated with allergies and fevers
of the flesh. Flesh out as much as you can about his past,
your past lives lived among roaming tribes, romantic

royalty, plundering pirates or tricky tricks. Obsess
over his handsome profile on social media sites you
wouldn't ordinarily frequent without an experienced
guide, instruction manual or some form of protection.
Frequently check your breath, your pulse, your email

and phone, your hair in anything reflective, with
the exception of his mirrored sunglasses. Dress for sex,
for success, to impress. Don't forget to wear clean

underwear. Remember what your mother told you about
reckless drivers and crosswalks. Cross with the light, cross
your heart and hope to die of embarrassment if he ever sees
you crossing your heart. Hide the doodles, the scrawled
hearts on binders and spiral notebook covers containing

GREGG SHAPIRO

the swirly equation of your initials in a place so secure
that even you have trouble remembering where it is. Cover
your ass. Remember, he doesn't even know you're alive.

MISS CUED

- *Allison Fradkin*

The first time we kiss, we are
wearing playbill-patterned pajamas,
blaring the soundtrack to *Starlight Express*,
and swearing off guys,
all of whom we've never cast an eyeball at
in the first place.

We've been too busy making eyes
at each other:
root beer float-brown
gazing at gumball-green.
Except now we're looking
at each other
just enough but not too much,
like actresses cheating out
to deliver dialogue.
Only we've both
gone up on our lines.
Or maybe we just haven't
learned them yet.

Eventually, we pick up our LGBT-cues
and the distance between us
starts to dwindle,
until your sugared grapefruit scent
and piggybank-pink pucker
are kissably close—
closer than a checker on a square.

I just can't wait to be kinged.
So I don't.
I lean in and latch on.
When it comes to kissing you,
there's no business like
slow business.

ALLISON FRADKIN

Everything about it is appealing:
the overture
that relevés into the opening number,
with its thoroughly modern melody;
the up-tempo standard
that grapevines into
the introspective piece,
rendered with restrained longing.

And when the power ballad pivots
into the emotional climax,
with its harmonically-held high notes,
one singularly sensational
kick line
starts inside my heart.

From the stereo, the cast launches into
"A Lotta Locomotion,"
and even though it's not
the locomotion,
we are definitely doing
a brand new dance now:
experiencing
something wonderful,
loverly,
and truly scrumptious.

Afterwards, we huddle in a cuddle
of ingénue giggles,
stage whispers,
and bass clef-style smiles.
We share the lyrical sentiments
that inspired our introductory intimacy:
I'm the bravest individual I have ever met,
Sweet Charity contributed.
I'd be surprisingly good for you,
evoked Evita.
I think I'm gonna like it here,
Annie averred.

"We're gay
and thespian,"
you remind me,
threading your fuchsia-frosted fingers
through my theatre curtain-colored ones.
"So what she really warbled was:
I think I'm gonna like it queer."

I try to reply, but the intermission
between our first kiss
and our second kiss
has ended on a high note.
The skate-shod *Starlight* singers
may be on a roll,
but this lip-locked lesbian is in a role:
your leading lady.

BECAUSE OF FACEBOOK

- *Gregg Shapiro*

My mother knows more about what I do in my personal life than I would ordinarily share with her. I know more about her social and romantic exploits than I ever cared to consider. However, learning

about ex-lovers' pursuits has not proven as disturbing as I thought it would be. Politically conservative cousins and acquaintances praise and throw their support behind homophobic and racist politicians and

pundits. Instead of unfriending them, I religiously follow their posts. It's better to know what your enemies are saying about you than to suffer plead ignorance. A former grade-school classmate apologized

for not coming to my defense when I was getting my ass kicked on a daily basis during recess or gym class dodgeball games. High school bullies gone to seed and their formerly cheery, now dreary, cheerleader

girlfriends, who wouldn't urinate on me if I was on fire in front of my locker, are now all up in my junk. I say, "You already took my lunch money. What more do you want from me?"

THE BOY

- Mykyta Ryzhykh

a boy in a sweater instead of a body
draws a tattoo instead of a mole

a boy with a voice instead of silence
wants to fill my chair with air

the boy with tears comes
into the room in which
I am not and fills
the chair in which
I am not sitting

my past passed in a chair
in my chair where I am no more

the boy lives in the past
and does not believe in the future

THE NEW STANDARD

- *Scott Wiggerman*

I was satisfied with a handcar,
with pumping the lever up and
down on my own like someone
in a silent movie, with working
my way down rusty tracks
to the nearest lonely station—
and then I crashed into you.

Now I want a shiny silver
railrunner, an aerodynamic
wonder that can go from Paris
to Moscow in five hours, time
enough to enjoy the dining car
with red velvet cushions and
white-gloved waiters who never
let my scotch glass fall below
the halfway mark. A private car
insulated from the rush of wind
and clatter of wheels, a car
where I can fall asleep in one
continent and wake in another,
a roomy car that makes other
compartments seem the size
of caskets, an era I'd rather forget.

Ah, but add a caboose for the sake
of nostalgia, one that looks back
at breath-taking mountain passes,
at hamlets where villagers wave
as if they wish they could board,
while the sun gleams like a blazing
ball of afterglow and the stream-lined
train lifts above the fog of past
destinations, its brash horn a strain
of music composed just for us.

SCOTT WIGGERMAN

(published in *Softblow,* April 2018)

ACHING

- BJ Louis

Armored boy with the blue eyes
golden lion locks
mythical in every way—
how he drapes himself
over me and consumes me. I swallow him
like cinnamon and cloves, cardamom,
warm honey, sweet figs
and plums. His face
under the moonlight
his skin slick wet in the sun
lemon light, crystalline back.
I beg him not to leave
I've gotten used to this warmth.

A LITTLE QUEER, TOO

i saw them open the one openly gay kid on the bus until he took his own life, and told myself that wasn't going to be me next; i was already bullied for so many things: being a loner, always writing or buried in a book, for being the favorite of some of my teachers, for not going to parties to underage drink—didn't want to be bullied for that, too, so i told a lie that i myself believed for entirely too long: "i'm straight as an arrow"; but i wasn't and i never was—i remember sitting in the church feeling like i was going to be smited down for being somewhere i didn't belong, those pews and those words offered me no solace or protection; i only liked when we were singing because of my love of words and stories and mythologies—none of them saw through my mask, but i was always afraid it was slipping; wondered if one of my celebrity crushes might give it away—but one day i was grown and met another young woman at my school that took my breath away, i learned at college i couldn't ignore who i was any longer; and yet i tried to bury it anyway still afraid of being judged or getting smited or even the concept of hell—it wasn't until i got my own apartment later that i realized that love is love, and society is the ugly one not me; i love with all my heart and all my soul and everything in me trying to make a better place for everyone in this world—my rainbow heart isn't the issue, i want to step out of the closet; to bask in the sunlight and the moonlight and every authentic in who i am—unafraid of judgment, unafraid of bullies, unafraid of God; because if we're all made in His image then he must be a little queer, too.

- *inda m. crate*

REALITY

- Abdulrazaq Salihu

Maybe, I'd wake
Into a seagirt
To swallow an island
On this yellow wallpaper.
Looking through them
I can see into the
Grave below, the dark brown
Of reality.
Soon— I might
Save my gullet a starch.
The simplest form,
Where the bully, after choking
My father's throat, has come to be.
Soon— I might fall inside.
I enter the grave the way
An island entered me—
By encroaching towards the
Thirst of this wide hungry mouth.

BLEEDING HEARTS

- Chris Biles

In the soil was planted fear
meant to flower into disgust and hate
so that their sense of right and wrong
became twisted like purple vines meant to suffocate
and we became something other than human:
green growths climbing skyward
but existing only to be ripped out by the roots
allowed to desiccate in the sun that would otherwise
provide sustenance

They were taught to see us as abominations,
emboldened by the bible, or by abhorrence, or by both.

Entitled men with sticks in their hands tend to use them
so that in protest you'll find
as they lean on theirs
you'll be beneath them
feeling the weight of your pride
in bruises
and blood

And then
pinned in the dirt
surrendering in the soil
it becomes hard to remember
that you haven't
         always
                 been
  a bleeding heart

ASYLUM SEEKER

- *Scott Wiggerman*

> *According to the American Immigration Council, fewer than 25,000 immigrants a year are granted asylum from as many as 600,000 open cases in the U.S. On average more than 1000 days go by while cases are pending. LGBTQ asylum seekers are usually required to show that treatment in their home country amounts to persecution on account of their LGBTQ identity.*

The echo in the garden
    heard through roots of the land,
but also the root that tastes
    of toil and ginger,
and the ginger seeped like raindrops
    into a cup of imperfect tea,
the cup with a permanent crack
    unseen in the terrine of night.

And the night of a shooting star
    that flames through a universe of indifference,
but also the universe found
    in the palm of a restless hand,
and the palm that flourishes
    unwatered in the desert,
the water that no one's tasted
    below the pocked surface of the moon.

And the moon whose influence
    makes minds muddy and mad,
the mud that barefoot children play in
    without thoughts of glass shards or gender,
but also the glass that refracts
    a rainbow of dazzling colors,
and strains of *Somewhere Over the Rainbow*
    like the echo of what's to be unearthed.

(Published in *22 Poems & a Prayer for El Paso*, Albuquerque: Dos Gatos Press, 2020)

NO SAY

- Chris Biles

Strings pull at your arms, legs
Strings reach in
through both ears
they wind their way along each fold and crevasse
of your brain
– tremble
because you have no say.

Strings stretch down
past clenched teeth
between your left tonsil and sensitive uvula, down
ridged esophagus and into your heart
Strings weave inside
both atria, both ventricles
veins, arteries
Your heart beats to the pull
of the strings
– tremble
because you have no say.

They decide
what is in your heart.

They decide
– so, tremble
because you have no say.

But, by God, be grateful.

CHAOS IN THE COSMOS

- *Chris Biles*

Something's missing
in all this empty space
as false hope
hangs heavy
in this so-called ordered universe.

Like so many
the parts of me
can't quite
click into place.

Can't. Won't.

I am the lid
to a broken box
sitting askew
uncomfortable
lamenting the fact
that I don't fit
that I can't keep safe
what lies within.

And you are too.

I am gears, turning
in some grinding machine, turning
turning until
that missing tooth
comes along
and then it all
comes crashing
down:
chaos in the cosmos.

And you are too.

CHRIS BILES

But it's okay.

The cosmos is
a Barbie doll universe.
If we're to be honest
nothing
can be so well-ordered.
If we're to be honest
there's more than one lost tooth
that will come along
there is no order to the timing
there is no order to the fall.
If we're to be honest
no box in this universe
has a lid that truly fits
because that definition
is different for us all.

We sit askew
boxes broken
there is space
between.

But it's okay.

Celestial bodies
        – bigger than us –
        – lifetimes longer than ours –
in their orbital dance
feel the pull
and the push
of billions of years
and there is so much space
for so much chaos
so just let go.

Just let go.

Time now to simply be
enraptured by the entropy.

RESURRECTION

- Scott Wiggerman

He calls me bear, a spirit animal
if you believe in such—not sure I can.

I don't believe in much. Not sure I can
follow the fetish of a dreamcatcher.

In dreams I fathom many a fetish.
I slither on the sheets like a rattlesnake.

I rattle when I anticipate his snake.
An ojo de díos opens on the bed.

A one-eyed oso, a god of the bed,
I growl as though awakening from winter.

I claw as though awakening with ghosts.
I rise with the hunger of months in a cave.

I rise hungry as Jesus three days in a cave.
He calls me bear, his spirit animal.

PERMA-VALENTINE

- Celia McClure

i.
My mother asks me to play a song that isn't about love,
and I scroll through gaudy pink album covers, struggling to find a song absent of pet names.
My friends ask me why I seem to only write love poems.
I beg the question,
what else is there?
If you know the answer, do tell,
for when the sun shines, I attribute it to Mother Nature's matronly heart,
I like to think that grass grows because it misses the morning dew.
And yes,
I admit,
I let my heart become a temple, convert beliefs a little more often than most.
The woman in New Orleans noted my heart-shaped glasses and the love inked on my thighs, and said "Your guides are telling me you're a being of love."
After an hour, sympathetic to my counterpart,
I asked
"Do you think we are all beings of love, but some of us are hindered and can't see it, can't express it?"
She replied like blood from the nose, "Well, of course."
Every poem I write is a love poem because love is our lifeblood,
it saturates moonshine and prosecco and the steam from morning showers,
it's what birthed bunnies and spiders and grumpy old men and screaming teen girls.
How could I write about anything but love when my life is filled with the breath of my sleeping lover, lemon-y pasta made by my friends, hearing my baby sister yell "Happy!" over and over as I throw her in the air.
Love keeps us going,
it lies in each part of us,
sometimes it's just harder to find.
There's nothing to write about in this world other than love.
I couldn't absolve my lovesick heart if I tried.

ii.
I am nothing if not a being of worship,
an unlikely culprit from a family of no organization.
My father used to tell me we were going to church,
and as I'd scramble for clothes that fit, clothes more expensive than $3.99,
my father would laugh and tell me we were going to the woods,
wear good shoes.
God is something you're born into,
and I was born in a pool in the living room of a college town apartment.
Nonetheless, obsession blooms inside my eyes,
I fall to my knees to pray to my lover's bodies,
finding sanctity in knobby knees, bitten nails, acne scars, and stretch marks.
I've been told that I'm always either in love or heartbroken.
I kiss and I charm and I cry.
I say, "This one is nicer to me," but the next summer I am a godless man once again.
If we are all made in His image, who am I if not adoring?
It fills my body, the sun, my cell phone, my friend's mouths,
it does no good to diagnose it,
I go to church every Sunday.

iii.
To fall in love with a darling's handwriting,
the fine blonde hairs unseen by the streetlamp's eye,
the green illuminated by the sun,
is to thank the itchy, toad colored grass for revealing itself,
to let the chill of wind ice your skin,
to blink snow out of your eyelashes in a single digit blizzard.
To thank the seasons for their scheduled arrival,
paper roses in every coffee shop because the wrinkle of another's eyes have woken you up.
No matter how cold, the sun in April is met with a celebrity's welcome.
My arms invite the warmth and I kiss the waves,
chopped short with craft scissors, thinking of the impossibly stubborn ends littering the sink like oak leaves in the fall,
where the bench we sat on the day you didn't kiss me once was.

EVEN IF NO APOLOGY WILL EVER BE ENOUGH

i was never brave enough to tell you
that i loved you, and it terrified me
when i discovered that i did;
because i knew it would be met with
rejection as you saw me as a sister
and had someone else to hold—

i still think of you often,
and i know i will always love you;

love is about appreciation
not ownership or control and sometimes
this aching in me is a wound but i think
of all the memories so bittersweet
and i am thankful for the lessons you taught me—

i know you are probably off painting
a new life with new people in your life,
but i wonder if i drift upon your focus;

i still remember your love of anita blake and lady utena—

still remember white roses were your favorite,
can still recall that evening we spent dancing at dracula's ball;
and i still remember the whisper of rose water which you
loved so well—

my gran said you were quite the character,
and my mother still asks about you;
i am still haunted by your ghost but i know it's my fault
she's here instead of you and i'm sorry even if
no apology will ever be enough.

- *linda m. crate*

LONG KISS

- Scott Wiggerman

We left the water-orb
for a better world, perhaps,
one where persuasion-sames
were purported to live
in perpetual dove-times.
Still, we looked down
from our star-jumper
with a twinge of sadness
as we headed to the sand-orb,
a place where no one is born
and no one ever leaves.
We knew the rules.

I was seven when I
went through the pink-tinge,
when my skin turned
the unavoidable color
of a day exposed to sky-heat.
Some turned as early as four,
some as late as twelve.
Like all persuasion-sames,
by sixteen we'd be star-jumped
to live among our kind
on the distant sand-orb.
I had a friend who tried
to bleach the pink-tinge;
his skin bore spot-blotches
that emphasized the color.
As the slogan-roads announced,
There's no turning back.

He never made it here,
but I think of this boy
these many years since he
was laid into an ash-crate.

SCOTT WIGGERMAN

Despite the many mouth-mats
entangled with my own,
it's his I think of as I climb
to the top of the inferno-hole.
The rules are clear about reaching
sixty-seven Jupiter-moons.
I'm ready to take my leap—
though I'd rather it be
into a lake on the water-orb,
hand in pink-tinged hand
with that boy before he was
spot-blotched, a boy who
has always held a place
in my timid blood-pump,
a boy whose kiss was fervent
as the down-taking he chose.

GROWTH//DECAY

- Celia McClure

The sun wakes me up, golden and warm, and for that one glorious instant, I am utterly unaware of who, where, what I am.
Then I feel your fingers laced in my hair, feel your cold cheek on my shoulder.
If I am lucky I will detangle myself from your grasp, slip out of white sheets, shake out any remnants of you left in my hair, start on coffee.
More often than not I flinch against the sun and feel you coil tighter, smell you from each angle, any flies that came to rest fleeing (an option I don't seem to have), before I lay as still as possible, my muscles tense when your breathless words refuse to hit my cheek, until you slither to the other side of the bed and I rush to the kitchen, bathroom, away.
I work with windows open and milky tea growing cold, silent but for the clacking of my keyboard.
Occasionally you'll slip a hand around my shoulder, run your hands across the warm body you were once familiar with, while I smile, wondering how your cold hands came to rest on the nape of my neck.
At night I'll crawl into bed where you wait, I don't know how you fill your time without sleep. I tell you of my day, tenderly stitching your body back to the morning prime, smoothing handmade creations onto your skin. I'll drink warmth, cup the heat in my hands, watch you tap a finger against the glass and look at me with disappointed, senseless eyes.
When I finally lay down I think I sleep as much as you, eyes staring out my window, watching each houselight flutter off, listening to the complete silence in my, sorry, our bedroom, feeling the dead weight of your limbs rest on my waist.
I don't remember how we got here, I know I must have chosen this, loved you (you whisper the words I adore you, I adore you, I adore you into my ear when you think I can't hear), because otherwise I have no explanation.
I know very little as of late, but one thing is for certain: someday the sun will shine through my little window, and your hands will be in my hair, wrapped around me, and I will not wake up. Vines will grow over us, my kitchen will rot, and maybe then you will finally sleep.

SEPARATION

- *Alice Rose*

i / miss / being your friend / now / we / are just lovers / and i love the touch / the skin / the noise / the feel / but / there is nothing / like staying up / until sunlight / only kissing / and talking / and talking / and talking / and laughing / and i love you / but i miss / when you called me / your best friend / and i love you / but / i wish / i knew / if i stuck in your mind / if you love me / beyond / the flowers / and the sex / and you love me / but you miss / when i was happier / when i wasn't so nervous / when i knew / you were my bitch / when i knew / you found me / exciting / and fresh / and pretty / my childhood / formed / by / the need / to be / less / now / i faint / and i fall silent / and i am / so lonely / around / my friends / who love each other / out loud / and / love me / in / solitude / i hope you all know / you are my lovers / and my friends / and my family / just like / the tulips / and the professors / and the shard of glass / that pierced me / through my lovers rug / my shin / wet with blood / more blood on the sheets / more blood on my pants / a pain / so familiar / i almost / taste / the iron /

WE WAKE UP IN THE SUMMER

- Celia McClure

My city has the kind of storm that makes religion nervous, and the jar I set out for rainwater flies off my roof.
It is glass and I am terrified.
I walk out to find it and it is not only whole, it is upright and half full.
I find 10 four-leaf clovers in one weekend.
My backyard can't decide if it wants to reek of death or not.
I brush a spider off of my little sister's belly onto my thigh, my dad says the air changed around me.
I'm falling in love with someone who has no idea.
I'm keeping so many secrets that don't belong to me that I find them in my dirty laundry basket.
My best friend wants to see me and I don't want my step mom to die.
I want to know what peonies smell like.
I want men to stop texting me after midnight.
I want to keep making jokes about hard drugs without people thinking I do hard drugs.
I want to hold my hand in between the buttons of a lover's shirt and feel them laugh at how happy I am.
I want to tell someone I love them without it terrifying me.
I want to float and I want to be able to go into hot tubs without passing out.

MY TRUE IDENTITY

it is hard to be proud
of yourself

when all of your life
you were taught
who you are is wrong,

they didn't like how
feral and fierce i was;
tried to teach me
how to be tamed but
i was determined to hold
onto whatever little pieces of
myself that i could—

was ashamed of my queer
identity so i hid in the bones
of straightness long past due,

sometimes i still do because
i don't always feel safe

being my authentic self;

yet i am really exhausted of hiding
my rainbow heart because all i
have ever tried to do was be there
for everyone and help in any way
that i could and remind everyone i
love that they are loved and worthy—

i wish they could feel as if i were
worthy of their love should they know
my true identity.

- *linda m. crate*

GAY PRIDE

- Scott Wiggerman

May we bike a wide expanse of untidy sands,
of outliers and isles of desert brush.

May we ride and ride, our eyes primed
to an iota of wild, a mite of wine

among the tumbleweeds and idle browns:
a bind of thriving cacti. Divine!

May we smile and find a vital prize,
a sign in the uncivilized silence,

a blooming lighthouse, a riot of pink fire,
our desired life, our private tribe.

May we ride inspired while our kind expires.
May we rise above the spineless of these times.

(published in *New Verse News*, June 11, 2017)

THE DYKE-CLARATION OF LESBI-INDEPENDENCE

- Allison Fradkin

We hold these truths to be self-evident:
that all individuals
on the spectrums of gender and sexuality
are created equal,
that cupid
is hardly a straight-shooter,
and that being queer
is no Sapph-faux pas.

MY QUEER GENERATION

- Maid Čorbić

I am surrounded by various people around me
I'm not afraid I'm a queer boy
Because it gives me the strength to cuddle
They realize that LGBTQ + is a good thing
And that each of us has equal rights
To live the way he wants and dreams

I think my generation knows
Always that the meaning of existence is
My reason is a sincere woven soul
Because I believe my existence
Yes, I make myself free

I consider myself a queer; it just bothers me
That people sometimes do not understand the attitude
Because it hurts me when they say I'm zero
Because they don't know my story
And that they just want to make me crazy

Maybe the story makes more sense
If I still don't see the light of day
I am a queer generation boy
Who loves justice and reconciliation
And I carry the flag of pride with pride

To be proud with pride, I only know
Yes, my time is running out
Yes, my happiness is always present
Because veto and hope give me a feeling
That I'm still worth it somewhere

My knowledge, my power and supremacy
Let love continue to build inner emotions
The queer generation and I are a member of LGBTQ +

MAID ČORBIĆ

Proud I proudly hold on to my colors
Because I am happy when I have what I dream of
And that is my freedom of speech and feelings!

HEAR ME OUT

- Allison Fradkin

I may be hard-of-hearing
but I've got pride
coming out of my ears.
That doesn't mean
communi-gay-tion
is always easy though.
I read lips, you read lipstick.
Let's hear it for the boy?
Here we go again.
I'll sing a different tune, thank you.
In fact, I'll tune you out.
Now don't tympanic—
it's no great hearing loss.
On the advice of Nellie Forbush,
I went and washed that man
right out of my hair and
eardrummed him out
of my dreams.
Sorry to hear that?
That's neither here nor there.
And now I think I'll
turn off my listening ears,
remove the cool-aid from the cups,
and hear what I want to hear—
something laudable,
not audible.
Because here's the deal:
I'm hear
-ing impaired,
I'm queer,
get…
Well, you've heard all this already.
Now hear this:
from here on out,
let's be all ears, not all fears;

ALLISON FRADKIN

let's differentiate, not differenti-hate.
If you don't,
you'll never hear the end of it.
Oh, you heard me loud and queer?
Good.
Glad to hear it.

SCARLET

- BJ Louis

It's been four years
and things have changed
and things have not.

The feeling—that feeling
of black rot dripping
from my open mouth

a stain on my ribcage
deep to the marrow
malignance, it comes

and goes as it pleases.
The black, the black
it wails.

But now I have you,
your skin like velvet
soft on mine

when you touch me—
when you kiss me
I taste iron and wine

on my tongue and your voice
is smooth, thick like cherry
syrup dripping from your lips

into mine

and it cures me.

REVERENCE FOR THEIR LAVENDER VALIANCE

(Dedicated to Alain and Everton)

- Bob McNeil

"Rights are not won on paper. They are won only by those who make their voices heard." —Harvey Milk

Back when the illiberal-brained reigned in the 1980s,
  Alain and Everton, no different than other gays in America,
  lacked alphabet-basic civil rights
  that certain idea-inflexible heterosexuals took for granted.

Back when the USA happily housed homophobia,
  xenophobia, racists, and sexists,
  Alain and Everton didn't halt.
  They trod the asphalt,
  seized the streets,
  made them purpose-filled platforms,
  and dared to air their need for democracy
  at Pride Day parades.

Back when Uncle Sam wouldn't mull
  the ever-growing hole in his hull,
  AIDS invaded marginalized lives
  unnoticed by myopic right-winged eyes.
  Long before high-classified communities realized
  the disease was a sniper aiming
  at anyone with a name,
  Alain and Everton were in the nation's forepart
  fighting for the illness-positive striving to live.

Back when it seemed like gloom entombed
  every bar, club, and tearoom,
  Alain and Everton, that pair of caring lovers
  saw purple patches appear on the fabric of their skin.
  Contrary to their disintegrating T-cells,
  their torn or tossed senses,

and their flower-wilting flesh,
they continued lobbing constitutional logic
at the United States of Apatheia
and its Mount-Rushmore-hard façade.

Back then, when success was star-far
and unattainable, that caring pair
remained dedicated to The Life,
and that caring pair was Out in the World
praying history would not dismiss
how they tried to create LGBTQ pride.

WHAT RETURNS?

- Mariel Cariker

When Right Whales migrate
they don't eat for an entire year.
They arrive to their feeding grounds
around Antarctica near starvation.
They've made it.
The Right whale was hunted to near
extinction, easy to harpoon
willing to come close to shore
vulnerable to strikes by large ships
or getting tangled in fishing wire.
Maybe I've always been most intrigued
by parts of this world
that are much bigger than me,
or maybe I'm prone to rooting for
the ones who stay close to the water's
edge willing to risk their lives
to get a good look at what's above them.
It is a gift to live your full lifespan.
Right whales can live up to 70 years,
researchers use their ear wax to determine
their age after they've died.
I didn't know whales had ears,
and although they all look the same from the
surface each whale has a white patch on its head
called a callousite
that's unique to each one.
Slow moving, patient, going from
breeding areas along the coasts
of Chile and Argentina,
Southern Africa, Australia
and New Zealand.
2,500 kilometers each way.
Named "Right" by the hunters
who hoped to kill them,
the Whales feast for months

and live off the fat accumulated for
the rest of the year.
But they always loop back.
They run themselves ragged for
their own good.
At their least nourished,
still majestic, still powerful
still overtaking the ocean.
Gliding through to where they
belong. Although they are gigantic
they are not a threat to people.
I want to be like the Right Whale,
or maybe I just want to be in the water with
one swimming through their giant ear canals
listening to the warbles
of the whale singing
looking for the rare others like it.
I want to be the Right anything,
to live off of what I provide myself
for longer than seems possible.
I want to defy expectation,
to always know I'm going home
eventually, slow moving,
patient
named Right even by those
who want me gone.

ABOUT THE AUTHORS

CHRIS BILES

Chris Biles is a queer writer/artist currently living and working in Washington D.C. She enjoys playing with the light and the dark, and losing herself in music, anything outside, and some words here and there. Published by Neon Door, Bourgeon Online, Exeter Publishing, Evening Street Review, Haunted Waters Press, Yellow Arrow Publishing, Signatures Magazine, FleasOnTheDog, Another New Calligraphy, and others. You can find her at marks-in-the-sand.com / Instagram: @marks.in.the.sand

MARIEL CARIKER

Mariel Cariker was born and raised in Westchester, New York and now resides in Somerville, Massachusetts after getting a degree in journalism and women's, gender and sexuality studies from Boston University. Her writing has been featured in Down in the Dirt Magazine.

AMB. MAID CORBIC

Maid Corbic from Tuzla, 22 years old. In his spare time he writes poetry that repeatedly praised as well as rewarded. He also selflessly helps others around him, and he is moderator of the World Literature Forum WLFPH (World Literature Forum Peace and Humanity).

LINDA M. CRATE

Linda M. Crate's works have been published in numerous magazines and anthologies both online and in print. She is the author of ten published chapbooks, four full-lengths, and three micro-chaps. She has a novella, also, called Mates (Alien Buddha Publishing, March 2022).

ALLISON FRADKIN

Allison Fradkin (she/her/hers) has a gay old time applying her Women's & Gender Studies education to the creation of satirically scintillating Sapphic poetry, prose, and plays. An enthusiast of inclusivity and accessibility, she delights in her day job of Dramatist for Special Gifts Theatre, adapting scripts for actors of all abilities; and her gay job of Literary Manager for Violet Surprise Theatre, curating new works by queer women, trans folx, and non-binary folx. Allison's auxiliary activities include vintage shopping, volunteering, and tending to her thespian tendencies.

BJ LOUIS

BJ Louis earned his MFA in Creative Writing from Hofstra University where he taught two undergraduate courses. As a proud member of the LGBTQ community, his coming of age writing consists of themes of gender and sexuality. His short fiction has been published in "Bloom" Literary Magazine, and his poetry can be read in numerous Red Penguin Collection anthologies. He is from Long Island, New York.

CELIA MCCLURE-SIKKEMA

Celia is a student at Grand Valley State University, studying Social Work and Women, Gender, and Sexuality Studies. They've been writing poetry since they could hold a pencil, and they've published four chapbooks previously, including 'teenage tryhard'. They like ghosts a lot.

BOB MCNEIL

Bob McNeil, writer, editor, cartoonist, and spoken word artist, is the author of Verses of Realness. Hal Sirowitz, a former Queens, NY Poet Laureate, called the book "a fantastic trip through the mind of a poet who doesn't flinch at the truth." Among Bob's recent accomplishments, he found working on Lyrics of Mature Hearts to be a humbling experience because of the anthology's talented contributors.

MARCH PENN

March Penn is a queer poet and founder of the Self-Educating Poets Network, a literary group providing free resources and meeting space to writers. Penn's poetry is published in What Are Birds, The Offing, The Fem and other literary magazines. Penn has featured in Boston at the Cantab Poetry Lounge and Stone Soup.

ALICE ROSE

Alice Rose is a poet located in West Michigan. They are a lover of plants, a decent kisser, and they're certainly trying their best.

MYKYTA RYZHYKH

Published in the journals "Dzvin", "Ring A", "Polutona", "Rechport", "Topos", "Articulation", "Formaslov", "Colon", "Literature Factory", "Literary Chernihiv", on the portals "Literary Center " and "Soloneba", in the "Ukrainian literary newspaper", the almanac "Syaivo".

ABDULRAZAQ SALIHU

Abdulrazaq Salihu is Nigerian member of the panel for The Nigerian Review, he's a poetry editor at Teen lit journal and a member of the hilltop creative arts foundation. He won the poetry category of the Nigerian prize for teen authors and was the first runner up for the prose category of the same prize in 2022. He won the splendors of Dawn poetry foundation poetry contest and has his works published internationally and nationally, he was the winner of the 2022 MASKS LITERARY magazine poetry award and is currently learning better ways to heal and exist as man. He can be found on twitter: @Arazaqsalihu;Instagaram, abdulrazaq._salihu

GREGG SHAPIRO

Gregg Shapiro is the author of eight books including the poetry chapbook Fear of Muses (Souvenir Spoon Books, 2022). Recent/forthcoming lit-mag publications include The Penn Review, Book of Matches, Sangam Literary Magazine, Exquisite Pandemic, RFD, Gargoyle, Limp Wrist, Mollyhouse, Poetic Medicine, Impossible Archetype, Red Fern Review, The Pine Cone Review, The MockingOwl Roost, and POETiCA REViEW, as well as the anthologies Moving Images: Poems Inspired by Film (Before Your Quiet Eyes Publishing, 2021), This Is What America Looks Like (Washington Writers' Publishing House, 2021) and Sweeter Voices Still: An LGBTQ Anthology From Middle America (Belt Publishing, 2021). An entertainment journalist, whose interviews and reviews run in a variety of regional LGBTQ+ and mainstream publications and websites, Shapiro lives in Fort Lauderdale, Florida with his husband Rick and their dog Coco.

SCOTT WIGGERMAN

Scott Wiggerman is the gay author of three books of poetry, Leaf and Beak: Sonnets, Presence, and Vegetables and Other Relationships; and the editor of several volumes, including Wingbeats: Exercises & Practice in Poetry, Bearing the Mask, and 22 Poems & a Prayer for El Paso, winner of a New Mexico/Arizona Book award. Poems have appeared in such journals as Gyroscope Review, Mollyhouse, Unlost, Shot Glass Journal, Red Earth Review, Rogue Agent, Limp Wrist, and Impossible Archetype. His website is: http://swig.tripod.com

ALSO FROM THE RED PENGUIN COLLECTION

POETRY

Words for the Earth – A Poetry Project
'Tis The Seasons – Poems to Lift Your Holiday Spirits
the flower shop on the corner – A Spring Poetry Anthology
the ocean waves – A Summer Poetry Anthology
the leaves fall – An Autumnal Poetry Anthology

FICTION

What Lies Beyond – Sci-Fi Stories of the Future
I Can't Find My Flashlight – Contemporary Campfire Stories
A Heart Full of Love – A Collection of Romantic Short Stories
Behind Closed Doors – A Mystery Anthology
Once Upon A Time… – A Fairy Tale Anthology
Ernest Lived …and other Historical Fiction Short Stories
Until Dawn – A Supernatural Anthology
Treat-or-Trick – Halloween Horror Stories
Pets On the Prowl – An Animal Mystery Anthology
My Robot & Me – A Not-So Fiction Anthology

THE STAND OUT SERIES

Stand Out – The Best of The Red Penguin Collection, Vol. 1
Stand Out – The Best of The Red Penguin Collection, Vol. 2